triple *A*s
for the
Soul

YOUR PATHWAY TO
PERSONAL FREEDOM

AGELESS✳WISDOM PUBLISHING
Palm Springs, California

Kent
Blanchard

Published by Ageless Wisdom Publishing
420 North Villa Court, Unit 202
Palm Springs, CA 92262

Orders: www.TripleAsForTheSoul.com

Cover Illustration and Design: Brogdon Design
Proofreading: Brenda Gunderson
Production Editorial: Dan Sause

Library of Congress Control Number: 2007904427

First Edition, November 2007
ISBN#: 978-0-9797-108-1-0

CONTENTS

ABOUT THE AUTHOR

LIFE COACH TRENT BLANCHARD, M.A. assists people in removing the obstacles that get in the way of living a life of fulfillment, joy and peace. He does this through individual Life Coaching, writing, workshop facilitation and public speaking engagements.

He received his undergraduate degree in Human Resource Management and spent over a decade in New York City in various Human Resource functions for major corporations. Trent holds a Masters degree in Spiritual Psychology and is a certified addiction counselor. He is also an ordained Interfaith Minister.

In his private practice, Trent works with clients mainly in Palm Springs and Los Angeles. However, as a result of his popular workshops, Trent works with individuals all over the country and regularly with at-risk youth.

Trent resides in Palm Springs, California where he is actively involved in his community.

INTRODUCTION

Many years ago, my spiritual therapist and mentor gave me a wonderful piece of advice. She said the best gift I could give the world was to heal myself. Through that statement, I realized I had spent many years trying to help others heal, when I wasn't doing it for myself. It was one of those "ah-ha" moments Oprah always talks about. My Spirit knew it was true and it changed my life. I then made the decision to dedicate my life to my own healing and from this healing came many blessings, including liberation from long standing suffering, finding happiness beyond measure, discovering a deeply satisfying and fulfilling career where I am of service to my fellow man, and the creation of this book, which details a practical path to finding personal freedom.

Triple A^s for the Soul

I share the stories of my own life with the intention of assisting you in healing yours. Regardless of your life experience, if you are now experiencing pain and suffering, this book will help!

I encourage you to focus not on the particulars of my stories, but the feelings and emotions underneath them which we can all relate through their universality. I hope this book will become a beacon of light which you can use to guide you on this sometimes painful and lonely journey. I pray that you have faith during the process, because if I could get through it, anyone can!

The book is broken down into twelve chapters, each containing an Article, an Affirmation, and various Action steps. I encourage you to focus on one chapter; read the article, recite the given affirmation, and then work with the suggested action steps until completed. **Do not move on until all action steps are completed!** I know you will find this process very powerful and beneficial.

Most importantly, I pray this book will help you remember the Truth of who you are; a Perfect,

INTRODUCTION

Divine, and Whole spiritual being having a human experience — not the other way around as some religions teach. When you shift your consciousness to embrace this Truth, personal freedom is inevitable!

Please note wherever I use the name God, I welcome you to replace it with the God of your understanding: *Higher Power, Source, Christ, Buddha, Beloved Creator, Spirit, One, Flow, Great Energy, Universe*, etc. In Truth there is only ONE source, having many names.

The very fact you have this book in your hands is a clear sign of your intention to move to a deeper level of awareness and healing within yourself. I acknowledge your courage in answering the call of your Soul.

I am profoundly honored, grateful, and blessed to be given the opportunity to share my story and be of service! Thank you, from the bottom of my heart!

ACKNOWLEDGEMENTS

I WOULD LIKE TO THANK Mona de Crinis for giving me a vehicle to be heard, Kimberly Nichols for her love and support in getting this book made, Rev. August Gold and Monica Blauner for their brilliant wisdom and guidance through the difficult times, and publisher Frank Callaghan for challenging me to make this book what it needed to be!

Deep gratitude goes to my family and beloved friends who have supported and loved me all through my life. I am eternally grateful to all of my earth angels.

triple A s
for the
Soul

YOUR PATHWAY TO
PERSONAL FREEDOM

CHAPTER ONE

*A*RTICLE: The Healing Journey

*"In order to have the inner peace we desire,
we must look at our perceptions about
our painful past experiences and
then re-perceive them."*

Triple *A's* for the Soul

AS I LOOK BACK OVER MY LIFE, I realize that my driving force, from a very young age, was to find inner peace. Most of my childhood included living with anxiety; being the middleman between fighting parents, constantly bickering with siblings, or acting as my mother's protector and confidant. This chaotic, dysfunctional environment took its toll.

In order to find, or as I now understand, re-discover the peace I deeply yearned for, it was suggested I heal the unresolved issues of my childhood. The problem was I didn't consciously realize I had any! I thought everyone grew up in such households and had the same issues. I should have known healing needed to take place when, as an adult, I was unable to watch family home videos without crying. I'm sure you can relate to moments like this.

Until this point, I did everything in my power to keep busy. Unbeknownst to me, this was a clever avoidance technique that kept me from the unsettling realization that I had stuff to deal with and that my intimate relationships were unhealthy, abusive and quite simply, not working. I remember thinking

The Healing Journey

I either had extremely bad luck with relationships, or perhaps, I was the problem. After all, the only one consistent thing in all of those relationships was me! I decided to start therapy and embarked on what I now call my "healing journey."

My therapist, Monica was absolutely wonderful. I felt safe, heard, validated, and acknowledged — regardless of what I said or did. It was amazingly freeing and deeply sacred. But unfortunately at the same time, since I had never allowed myself to feel any of the negative emotions associated with my upbringing, I was overwhelmed with sadness, pain, and resentment. I felt as though I was in hell! This process was painful, tedious, long, and expensive, and yet, I persevered. Somehow I had faith everything was happening for a reason and felt in my heart it was necessary in order to find the inner peace I so deeply desired.

I was giving voice to the painful feelings I had buried deep inside while simultaneously reviewing the values, morals, and beliefs I learned, inherited and acquired from my family, society, and religion.

Therapy afforded me the opportunity to look at these beliefs, determine if they were working for me, then update or discard them accordingly.

After some time, I began seeing the fruits of my labor. My emotions were becoming more balanced and my familial relationships dramatically improved. It was at this time when someone suggested joining *The Artist's Way* workshop, based on the book written by Julia Cameron, which focuses on rediscovering creativity and joy. This workshop set in motion the process of integrating all of the parts of my life, the good and the bad, as well as the joy and the pain.

In addition, this program began the ever-important process of looking at my limited perception of God and how that was affecting my life. I heard for the first time, words that I now know without a doubt to be true; "we are spiritual beings having a human existence, and as such, are made Perfect, Divine, and Whole, in the likeness of our Creator." I began to see that forgetting this Truth was the root of all pain and suffering, including my own. As I began to meditate on this idea, my life began to transform!

I took full responsibility for my life, which greatly empowered me and, as a result, I am able to empower and inspire others to do the same. Because I now remember who I am, I spend time and energy focusing on my Truth, allowing me to experience more joy, gratitude, and love in my life. This is not to say I don't have bad days, but the difference is that my healing journey has equipped me with gentle tools and techniques to deal with the issues when they resurface and get me back to the Truth of who I am quicker and the "forgetting time" is shorter!

To go one step further, I am blessed with the awareness to look at those past situations in a different way, which allows me to view every experience in my childhood as a blessing because it has prepared me for my true work in this world — being of service to others as they walk their own healing journeys.

From this experience, I have learned many things. In order to have the inner peace we desire, we must look at our perceptions about our painful past experiences and then re-perceive them. We must take responsibility and control of our lives by figuring out why those things happened *to* us, or better yet happened *for* us and find our purpose in life. We must learn that in order to truly heal our lives, we need to heal our thoughts, because the thoughts that we focus on create our life experience; focus only on the positive thoughts and your life will change for the better! To elaborate on this concept, I use the words of Patrick Overton, "Watch your thoughts; they become words. Watch your words; they become actions. Watch your actions; they become habits. Watch your habits; they become character. Watch your character; it becomes your destiny."

But most importantly, we must remember who we Truly are, children of God with unlimited potential; we must begin the journey of correcting the thinking that is not in alignment with that Truth! We will be discussing each of these points in detail throughout this book.

I have been blessed to hear how sharing my stories have benefited others. They give hope, inspiration, and encouragement to persevere on the journey of self-discovery! This, too, can be your experience if you read on! How exciting is that?

I now invite you, dear reader, to commit to your own healing journey. Although your issues may look different than mine, you have picked up this book for a reason. Let's embark together on the process of remembering and do the work necessary to get back in alignment with that very initial Truth — that we are spiritual beings having a human existence.

$\mathcal{A}$FFIRMATION

"I am ready for healing and transformation."

$\mathcal{A}$CTION STEPS

1. Find a special place in your home and perform a ritual dedicating it as your "sacred, safe space." This will be a retreat for you to remember, heal, dream, learn, unlearn, grow, and unfold!

2. Buy yourself a special journal and dedicated writing instrument, and enter today's date. This will become a sacred record of your healing journey.

3. Write the word COURAGE in big letters on the first page. Let it act as a reminder of the great courage you are showing by walking this journey of self-discovery!

4. Copy the suggested affirmation and post it in visible places to help you remember it throughout the day! Recite it numerous times every morning and evening.

5. Write in your journal any negative, doubtful thoughts that come up while reciting the affirmation. These thoughts are fear and the process for dealing with them will be addressed in Chapter Five.

6. Break down your life into 5 year increments, 0-5, 6-10, etc. For each increment, write down the situations you feel are unresolved, that bring you pain. We will revisit this list in Chapter Four. In the meantime, trust that following the *Triple A*^{s} *for the Soul* pathway, you will find healing and resolution.

7. Write down your definition and current understanding of God. Complete the sentence; God equals _____! If your God is one of limitation, judgment, or fear, you are still dealing with a god consciousness that has remained unexamined since childhood, which is toxic. This must be updated to God is unlimited and unconditional love!

CHAPTER TWO

ARTICLE: Conscious Breath Work

*"When we are in the present moment,
we have everything we need, lack nothing,
and have the experience that all is well."*

Triple $\mathcal{A}$s for the Soul

AFTER WALKING MY HEALING JOURNEY for a couple years, I transitioned from my traditional therapist to a spiritual counselor, Rev. August Gold. During my first session, I shared with August what was, or perhaps more relevant, what was not working in my life. She listened with empathy and compassion to my stories, but I sensed she wasn't especially interested in the details. Without actual words, I was beginning to understand that my "story" was simply a story that I myself created based on my perception of what happened and I didn't have to buy into it anymore. I could create a new story that worked better for me. A moment later, she informed me that our work together was to get to the root of the problem which begins by returning to our natural state as human beings found through our breath!

She taught me "breath work," a deep and conscious series of inhales and exhales. In the process of focusing on the breath, on each and every inhale and exhale, I was instantly escorted back to the present moment, where inner peace, calm, and centeredness resided! It was delicious and freeing. From this brief, yet profoundly powerful experience, I knew my life was going to change.

The simple act of silent breathing refocuses our minds on the present. Many of us have been focusing on the unhappy events that happened in the past, and consequently project similar outcomes onto future events that have not yet happened, which brings us great suffering and depression. Remember the concept discussed in the previous chapter that says the thoughts we focus on create our life experience!

When we are in the present moment, we have everything we need, lack nothing, and have the experience that all is well, bringing us back to our natural state as spiritual beings — Perfect, Whole, and Divine! This place is our birthright and, thankfully, is only a deep inhalation away. Our task is to remember this from moment to moment.

This experience helped me realize that a large part of my job was helping others rediscover this place within themselves! I therefore begin all of my counseling sessions, workshops, and seminars with what I call "conscious breath work," my version of what I was taught on that sacred day in Augusts' office.

I added the word "conscious" to the technique because we unconsciously breathe without aware- ness most of our lives. Thankfully, our brain auto- matically instructs the body to take in and release oxygen through the breath, which is usually short and shallow. Through this new technique of adding awareness to the process, we take in longer, more enriching breaths and use focused attention to fos- ter a sense of grounding and peace within.

The first step on your own journey towards healing is as simple as learning how to get present through conscious breath. There is no wrong way to do it; all you need do is notice your breathing. With this in mind, find a comfortable place to sit, plant your feet firmly into the ground, close your eyes, and bring your attention to your breath. Gen- tly take in a long, deep breath through the nose, imagining your chest expanding outwards, filling- up with as much clean, revitalizing, refreshing air as possible. Then, slowly exhale through the mouth letting go of anything in your body and consciousness that brings you discomfort, anxiety, or upset. Repeat this as many times as necessary, three times being the minimum. If you find yourself having a thought unrelated to your breath, notice the thought and simply return focus back to your breath. When you are finished, open your eyes and notice the difference in how you feel; my guess at the very least is more relaxed and grounded. It really is as simple as that!

Once you have experienced the benefits, I encourage you to incorporate this exercise into your daily routine. I suggest doing conscious breath work before taking your daily vitamins or medication, before walking out your front door or prior to eating any meal. By associating it with everyday activities, you remind yourself to practice and create a healthy habit for yourself.

The more noticeable results, however, come from using this technique when you find yourself in a stressful situation or feeling overwhelmed, such as directly following an upsetting disagreement or prior to returning a difficult phone call. It will quickly bring you back to center and balance, which enables you to think more clearly and respond accordingly.

You can also do an abridged version of this exercise when you find yourself getting agitated, irritated, or anxious in public, such as while waiting in line at the grocery store or sitting in your car at a stoplight. Once you have the awareness of the power of this tool, you will begin noticing how often you forget to consciously breathe and how wonderful and beneficial practicing it can be.

It is with great joy that I pass on this powerfully practical technique to you, for it is one of the greatest gifts I have ever received. Set the intention right now to do it regularly! When you do, you will find a peace, tranquility, and centeredness you never thought possible and will notice a positive change in your life.

*A*FFIRMATION

*"Breath brings me to the present moment,
where peace resides."*

*A*CTION STEPS

1. Practice "conscious breath work" every waking hour on the hour throughout the course of your work in this chapter. I suggest setting a wrist watch, palm pilot, or cell phone to remind you. This might seem daunting at first, but is necessary to re-program your consciousness with healthy behaviors.

2. Utilize conscious breath work whenever you find yourself upset, off center, or unbalanced.

3. Copy the suggested affirmation and post it in visible places to help you remember it throughout the day! Recite it numerous times throughout the day, and write in your journal any negative, doubtful thoughts that come up while reciting the affirmation. These thoughts are fear and the process for dealing with them will be addressed in Chapter Five.

CHAPTER THREE

ARTICLE: Remembering Truth

"Within each of us there is that holy spark of God which makes us at our very core Perfect, Divine and Whole."

Triple A's for the Soul

ACCORDING TO THE KABBALAH, the mystical teachings of the Jewish tradition, at some point at the beginning of time, the Holy was broken into countless pieces, scattering God sparks throughout the Universe. This belief, also found in the Hindu religion through its salutation "Namaste, The Divine spark within me honors the Divine spark within you," implies that God can be found in everything, including you and me.

Within each of us there is that holy spark of God which makes us at our very core Perfect, Divine, and Whole, a belief that is further supported in the Christian and Buddhist traditions which states we are all created in God's image and likeness. So, if our Creator is Perfect, Divine, and Whole, then so are we!

The problem is we have collectively forgotten this Truth — the Truth of who we are! Since childhood, we listened to other people's thoughts and beliefs and gave them more credibility than our own. We were constantly told that we needed to learn, change, or alter something in order to be "perfect," which would make us worthy of being loved and accepted. We then took these opinions on as our own and created from them our personal core belief system and hence have thoughts and feelings that support them.

However, our inner turmoil has been telling us that something isn't right; our lives aren't working because our belief system is based on the perspective of others and is in direct opposition to our personal Truth. It is a vicious cycle that you can't afford to buy into anymore. It needs to be changed.

We can begin by updating our perspective of what perfection is. When we look deeper at the word perfect, we find it is translated from the Greek "teleios," which more accurately means "fully complete or lacking nothing essential to the whole." Being perfect then, doesn't have as much to do with society's definition which focuses on making up for what we are lacking physically, but instead on the spiritual fact that we are whole and fully complete just as we are! You will realize when you begin changing this limiting perception, your true inner self will breathe a sigh of relief and unleash incredible healing within.

With this new and improved view of perfection, we are given the opportunity to look at ourselves through different, more accepting eyes. We start acknowledging we are Perfect, Divine, and Whole, which will allow us to be more compassionate and gentle with others because we are treating ourselves with those same qualities. We begin the important process of taking inventory of our God given talents, which enable us to share them with the world in a way that is unique and special only to us. This truly is our mission on this planet, beautifully stated in *A Return to Love* by Marianne Williamson "We were born to make manifest the glory of GOD within us. It is not just in some of us; it is in EVERYONE." We will come to understand we have everything we need inside ourselves and can embark on taking the necessary actions to have them come into being. This will be addressed in detail in Chapter Eleven.

Furthermore, according to *The American Heri-*

tage® *Dictionary of the English Language*, remembering is defined as, "a return to an original shape or form after being deformed or altered." We see that society's limited definition of perfection has deformed and altered us from our Truth, and led us astray from our original state of being. We need to return to Truth! Through remembering, or bringing back to wholeness who we truly are, we free ourselves from the chains that formerly were used to bind us.

How can you practically work on remembering Truth? Create the affirmation, also known as a statement of Truth, "I am Perfect, Divine, and Whole," and place it everywhere; on sticky pads near your computer, on your car dashboard, on your bathroom mirror. Say it out loud whenever you see it; even if at first you don't believe it true, just continue on and eventually you will believe. The more we remember this fact, the more we can focus our valuable energy on things that truly matter!

Another idea is to place a picture of yourself as a youngster on your bed stand and every morning and night, speak your affirmation directly to the child in that picture — your inner child. This will help him/her remember the Truth of who he/she really is, or quite possibly the opposite might occur; that child will help you, the adult, remember what he/she has always known true, but you, the adult, forgot in the process of growing up! When we truly get down to it, this journey is not about learning anything new, but about unlearning what you have learned that is not true!

It is our birthright to have happiness, joy, and peace in our lives. We move closer to these states of being by remembering the Truth, that we are Perfect, Divine, and Whole beings of light, created in God's image. It is up to us to remove the obstacles that stand in the way of achieving this goal; which we discover are our very own self-limiting beliefs and thoughts.

How exciting that you are embarking on the journey of remembering the Truth of who you are. It is our perception of our lack, not the Truth of our

wholeness, that holds us back from having everything we truly desire!

$\mathscr{A}$FFIRMATION

"I am Perfect, Divine and Whole."

$\mathscr{A}$CTION STEPS

1. Practice "conscious breath work" at least once in the morning, once mid-day, and once at night. Utilize conscious breath work when you find yourself off-center.

2. Copy the suggested affirmation and post it in visible places to help you remember it throughout the day! Recite it numerous times throughout the day and write in your journal any negative, doubtful thoughts that come up while reciting the affirmation. These thoughts are fear. Hold tight; the process for dealing with such thoughts will be addressed in Chapter Five.

3. Frame a picture of yourself as a child that represents joy and innocence and place it next to your bed. If you don't have a childhood photo handy, flip through magazines and find a picture of a child who can represent you.

4. First thing in the morning and last thing at night, spend a minimum of 5 minutes talking with your inner child and sending him/her love, compassion, and strength, reminding him/her of their Perfection, Divinity, and Wholeness. As the child within heals, so does the adult.

CHAPTER FOUR

$\mathcal{A}$RTICLE: Self Forgiveness

*"I forgive myself for judging others for hurting me,
because the Truth is I was actually hurting myself
by believing my own self-limiting beliefs."*

Now that you are well on the path to remembering who you Truly are and have been taught a practical and effective way to get connected to that peaceful, loving energy within yourself through breath, it's time to discuss the concept of forgiveness and begin the process of looking at your perceptions of the past and the influence they have held over you.

First, we must understand that everyone in life who you perceived hurt you, was doing the best they could, given their upbringing, and recognize they would have done better if they could have. A wise person once said "suffering and pain come when you are holding onto something that you need to let go of." To end such suffering, we need to stop blaming others and work, not on forgiving them, but instead, forgiving ourselves.

We begin this process by looking at your perceptions of the situations you've experienced throughout your life that bring you upset and then look at them from a different view. What might help you understand this is the quote, "People do not do things TO us, but do things FOR themselves." When I heard this, I instantly viewed my entire past experience in a different light and was able to shed the victim role.

I learned the only thing I could change about my past was my perception of it! I began to understand it wasn't about what happened to me, but instead how I viewed it. I welcome you to apply the same concept to your experiences. You will stop judging the actions of others and grasp the concept that they were doing what they had to do for themselves; it quite frankly had nothing to do with you. This doesn't make others past actions or behaviors right, but you can at least shed light on where they might have been coming from, hence making the situation somewhat understandable. It is a very liberating thought, because you are freed from the painful belief that their behavior was somehow a result of your lack, your unworthiness or your un-lovability.

With this understanding, forgiveness of others is inevitable because you realize they didn't consciously or deliberately do anything wrong. You will comprehend that someone who acted in such a way is in need of compassion, for those who do acts of anger and violence are in fact so deeply miserable inside that they have to hurt others to release the pain. After all, "hurt people hurt!" Consequently, you might even move into a place of compassion and empathy for the very people whom you have resented for so many years. This gives you a new found sense of power, freedom, and liberation.

Don't be surprised if you feel anger come up, for as you realize you don't need to forgive others, you might turn inward and become angry at yourself for falling prey to a lifetime of false beliefs that you yourself created which are in direct opposition to your birthright as a Perfect, Divine, and Whole child of God! Be super gentle and compassionate with yourself during this time because you didn't know about this Truth at the time you created such beliefs. I encourage you to apply a process called self-forgiveness.

The self-forgiveness process begins with closing your eyes, taking a deep conscious breath, placing your hands over your heart and repeating the following statements "I forgive myself for judging myself as less than, because the Truth is I am Perfect, Divine, and Whole!" or "I forgive myself for judging others for hurting me, because the Truth is I was actually hurting myself by believing my own self-limiting beliefs."

Once completed, you will feel liberated and will be in a place of true power and accountability, poised to reach those long-lost dreams. You have stopped blaming others and have begun the process of forgiving yourself. You have removed the self-defeating beliefs and thoughts that have kept you in chains and understand the real issue is that you betrayed yourself, and continued to do so, by believing the false ideas you created due to those situations.

True forgiveness is self-forgiveness, which is an inside job. If you are experiencing suffering and pain in your life, I encourage you to ask yourself where you might have betrayed yourself by denying the Truth of who you are and quickly move into self-forgiveness; the more you practice, the more effortless the process becomes. Once you do, you will find a calm and serenity that you have never before experienced. Self-forgiveness brings true freedom, because we finally forgive ourselves for judging ourselves for being anything less than the Perfect, Divine, and Whole spiritual beings that we are!

*A*FFIRMATION

"I forgive myself for judging myself as anything less than Perfect, Divine, and Whole."

*A*CTION STEPS

1. Practice "conscious breath work" at least once in the morning, once mid-day, and once at night. Utilize conscious breath work when you find yourself off-center.

2. Copy the suggested affirmation and post it in visible places to help you remember it throughout the day! Recite it numerous times throughout the day, and write in your journal any negative, doubtful thoughts that come up while reciting the affirmation. These thoughts are fear and the process for dealing with them will be addressed in the next chapter.

3. Make a list of those things you feel you need to forgive yourself for. To help you with this, review your journal and find the exercise in Chapter One, Action Step #6 that instructed you to break down your life into 5 year increments and identify the areas that need healing.

4. Practice self-forgiveness around the things you judged yourself and others for. Close your eyes, taking a deep conscious breath, placing your hands over your heart and repeat a statement such as "I forgive myself for judging myself as less than, because the Truth is I am Perfect, Divine, and Whole!"

5. Be gentle with yourself and acknowledge your willingness to do such courageous work.

CHAPTER FIVE

_A_RTICLE: Thoughts as Clouds

"You don't need to believe everything you think."

THROUGH THIS BOOK, we have come to understand much of the suffering we have experienced in our lives has been a result of forgetting the real Truth of who we are! Now that we are affirming what is true and forgiving ourselves and others for the many things we have judged and blamed them for, let's discuss another thing that, up until now, has controlled our lives and brought us a great deal of this pain; our negative core beliefs and the thoughts that support them.

As children, we didn't have the opportunity to consciously choose our own belief systems. We didn't know we had the power to decide which beliefs we wanted to believe or not. We were immersed with the morals, values, and beliefs of our parents, caregivers and society at large, which created our belief system, molded us into the people we are today and hence dictates the way we relate to ourselves and others.

The problem is that many of the things we learned from others, and the resulting thoughts that are caused by believing them, go against our own true nature. It is crucial that we examine all of the beliefs in our consciousness and determine if they are working for us; and since you have this book in your hands, my guess is a large majority of those beliefs do not work, and perhaps never did.

I recently heard a startling fact that 95% of the beliefs we hold and thoughts we think are negative and not true. WOW — that's a lot of "junk" hanging around in our minds! If we want true freedom from suffering, we must discard the ones that don't support our Perfection, Divinity, and Wholeness! Period! Let's begin that process now!

A practical way to identify that a negative core belief or thought is present is when you find your inner peace disturbed: whenever you feel a pit in your stomach, your heart beating at a very rapid rate, your palms getting sweaty, or shortness of breath or quickened speech. Your body has immense wisdom because it houses your Spirit, and since our birthright is peace, we best listen to it and correct any thinking that pulls us away from that peaceful state of being. The true healing that needs to occur in our lives is in **correcting our thinking**!

I once saw a bumper sticker that instantly gave me great freedom and relief, "You don't need to believe everything you think." I had never heard such a concept and was amazed when I realized I was the one creating my consistent state of mental exhaustion by giving energy to every single thought I had, with the majority of them being negative. No wonder I always felt tired. Focusing on my negative thoughts was producing a life experience that was primarily negative. I had the power to change my life by changing what thoughts I focused on. Way cool!

The power of this statement is this; if you focus only on the thoughts that are positive and support your magnificence, your life will become more positive and joyful. Why? Because you are affirming the Truth of who you are! In the beginning, watching your thoughts can be tedious and mentally exhausting, but you will soon begin experincing the beneficial results. This work actually becomes a labor of love!

How do you deal with your negative thoughts? It is quite simple; when the negative thought comes into your mind, simply observe it. Don't focus on it. Don't give it energy; let it pass on by. Think of your negative thoughts as clouds in the sky; there is one, there goes one, and another, and yet another. While observing a thought that is self-defeating, you can also quietly recite "Thanks for sharing" which neutralizes its affect and allows it to continue moving on!

Another great tool used in examining your core belief system is the book *The Four Agreements* by Don Miguel Ruiz. This book assists people in clearing out the thousands of beliefs, what Ruiz calls "agreements" that we pick up through our lifetimes and helps narrow them down to four simple ones that affirm Universal or Toltec Truth, quiet similar to the concepts in this book.

Core beliefs and the resulting negative thoughts that are created by them have run our lives long enough! Begin the process of reviewing and updating your core beliefs, begin to give energy only to those thoughts that bring you joy, and you will immediately begin experiencing liberation from self-imposed limitation.

*A*FFIRMATION

"I am aware of my thoughts and focus on those that bring me joy and peace."

*A*CTION STEPS

1. Practice "conscious breath work" at least once in the morning, once mid-day, and once at night. Utilize conscious breath work when you find yourself off-center.

2. Copy the suggested affirmation and post it in visible places to help you remember it throughout the day! Recite it numerous times throughout the day, and journal about the doubtful, negative thoughts that come up while reciting the affirmation.

3. Apply the following negative core belief/thought correcting process to each negative thought.

4. Take each thought and create a reframe statement/affirmation that is in alignment with the Truth of who you are; Perfect, Whole, and Divine! For example, if you had the thought "I am never going to have inner peace," create an affirmation that states, "Inner peace is my birthright." Another example, "I am unworthy" becomes "I am worthy of having whatever I desire."

5. Review your past journal entries and find your responses to the previous chapters Action Step where you journaled your doubtful, negative thoughts that came up while reciting the daily affirmation. Apply the above thought correcting process to each self-defeating thought. This can be a lengthy process, but the benefits are great. Give yourself plenty of time.

6. Identify 5 beliefs that no longer serve you — the things you believe true, but disturb your inner peace and calm when you think about them.

7. One belief at a time, look in the mirror and have a discussion with yourself about why the belief is not the Truth and explain the updated belief that will now be operating!

CHAPTER SIX

*A*RTICLE: Self Love

*"The beauty of self-love is that once you
love yourself, you are truly ready and able to
love others and fully embrace the
love others give you!"*

Triple A^3 for the Soul

IN THE LAST CHAPTER, we learned suffering comes when we focus on our self-defeating thoughts that do not bring us peace and we began the process of updating them. In addition, we discovered anxiety, discontent, boredom, and depression, all variations of suffering, result when we focus on the things we do not have in our lives versus acknowledging the things we do! This is particularly relevant when speaking of love, the thing that makes the world go round, the stuff that makes life worth living!

Up until now, many of us have concentrated on the love that is lacking in our lives instead of focusing on the abundance of love we have through our family and friendships. We say everything would be perfect if I just found that special person! However, if we were to take conscious inventory of our relationships and feel the love we now receive from these people, we would immediately feel a shift inside and would experience great joy and gratitude. By doing this, we would be able to see that our lives are perfect just the way they are because love already exists! Here it is important to state "love and fear cannot occupy the same space," so if you are feeling blessed by focusing on the love you have, you literally cannot, at the same time, feel depressed for the love you don't.

The real problem comes when you don't truly love yourself! If you don't love yourself, you will not be able to recognize what love feels like and be unable to experience it from others. Many times, the reason we desire an intimate relationship with another is because we do not know how to love ourselves and look for that love externally from another. This is a great tactic that can work for a while, but will always lead you back to that inner emptiness! You find true love, first and foremost, through loving yourself!

How do we love ourselves? A good way to begin this process is to stop every time you pass a mirror and repeat the statement "I love you" to yourself. Experience the feelings inside brought forward via your loving words. Be aware of the doubtful, negative thoughts that come up while you make this statement and then apply the negative thought correction process learned in the previous chapter.

I also recommend writing the affirmation "I am love and lovable" and place copies in various locations around your house or work, which will serve as a great reminder to love yourself throughout the day. The written and spoken word is extremely powerful when working on loving yourself! As Don Miguel Ruiz says in his book *The Four Agreements*, "It is through the word that you manifest everything. The word is a force; it is the power you have to express and communicate, to think, and thereby to create the events in your life."

However, many do the aforementioned exercises but then turn around and choose relationships and situations that do not honor themselves and are far from loving. The way we learn self-love is in part through word, but more importantly, through action.

What actions show self-love? What does an act of self-love look like? High on the list is finding someone who can help you deal with life's challenges and can assist you in looking beyond your limiting perceptions and beliefs. Albert Einstein once said "The significant problems we face cannot be solved at the same level of thinking we were at when we created them." For me, this was challenging as it involved spending money on myself which was something I had difficulty doing. My investment in the therapeutic process was one of the greatest gifts I have ever given myself and was the first action towards my own self-loving. If you cannot afford a personal therapist, be aware that many religious, spiritual, and community organizations offer low cost counseling alternatives. Make sure to always ask for credentials, seek testimonials from other clients, and listen to your intuition that tells you if the person is a right fit!

Another act of self-love is surrounding yourself with a community of like-minded people who love and support you unconditionally. This can often be found through attending spiritual or church services. Through such programs, we typically recognize one of the reasons we lack love in our lives is not only that we don't love ourselves, we are not fully connected with the God of our understanding, and are not able to experience the highest form of love that comes from the One who created us!

The process of loving yourself also includes taking inventory of the relationships in your life that are unhealthy and destructive. It might be time to release the ones that no longer serve you! A good yardstick in determining how you are doing in this area is to look at the relationships you currently have in your life. Are they based on unconditional love and respect? Do they honor your feelings and support you? What they are doing, or not doing, directly reflects what you are doing, or not doing for yourself. Make the decision right now to set the bar higher within yourself and not let anyone treat you in ways that you wouldn't treat yourself, and vice versa. Let this exercise simultaneously serve as a check to make sure you are being the type of friend you ideally desire!

In addition, giving yourself things your heart desires is self-loving: going to the gym, visiting a museum, eating a healthy diet, going on picnics, regularly buying fresh-cut flowers, taking personal time for yourself, or getting regular massages, pedicures, or manicures. Notice many of these activities do not involve spending large amounts of money! When you love and care for yourself first, you then show up more fully present for others, without resentments, which benefit everyone involved.

The beauty of self-love is that once you love yourself, you are truly ready and able to love others and fully embrace the love others give you! We discover through this process that we didn't need to find love because it was never lost; it was there all along! It was our limited perception of it that was the problem.

I encourage you to take time to focus on the love that exists in your life: the love of self, the love of friends and family, the love of the God of your understanding, and of course, love of your significant other if you have one. Shower yourself, and them, with focused love, special attention and thoughtful gifts. You will instantly feel love and will feel loved.

You will realize that you lack nothing, which brings you back to the state you were born to live in!

$\mathcal{A}$FFIRMATION

*"I show love to myself through my
loving thoughts and actions."*

$\mathcal{A}$CTION STEPS

1. Practice "conscious breath work" at least once in the morning, once mid-day, and once at night. Utilize conscious breath work when you find yourself off-center.

2. Copy the suggested affirmation and post it in visible places to help you remember it throughout the day! Recite it numerous times throughout the day, and write in your journal any negative, doubtful thoughts that come up while reciting the affirmation.

3. Apply the negative core belief/thought correcting process to each, as discussed in the previous chapter.

4. Every time you pass a mirror, repeat "I love you" to yourself. Be aware of the doubtful, negative thoughts that come up while you make this statement and then apply the same thought correction process to each thought, as discussed in the previous chapter.

5. Make a list of the people in your life who love you and focus on the gratitude of being blessed with such love.

6. Make a list of those relationships in your life that are unloving, unhealthy and no longer work. Hold tight; we will discuss how to handle this list in Chapter Ten.

7. Perform one small self-nurturing act daily. Ideas include going to the gym, drinking more water, eating a healthy piece of fruit, or taking personal time for yourself.

8. Perform one larger self-nurturing act weekly. Ideas include getting a massage, going on a picnic, treating yourself to a nice dinner out, or allowing yourself to do nothing but relax for one entire day without e-mail, phone, or contact with others!

CHAPTER SEVEN

ᴀRTICLE: Feelings lead to Healing

*"Anytime your peace is disturbed internally,
you have a choice to heal a core belief or
thought that is bringing you dis-ease!"*

Triple $\mathcal{A}$s for the Soul

HAVE YOU EVER HAD SOMEONE cut you off while driving down the street and witnessed yourself fuming with anger? Have you ever been on the phone with a customer service representative when they discredit something you said and find yourself yelling at the top of your lungs? Have you ever watched a movie and felt as though you could cry for days with sadness? If the answer to any of these questions is YES, read on!

These emotional outbursts are signs that your internal alarm system is going off, warning you that something needs to be addressed within your consciousness! As I have mentioned before, your body has immense wisdom because it houses your Spirit, which knows the Truth! Anytime your peace is disturbed internally, you have a choice to heal a core belief or thought that is bringing you dis-ease. I encourage you to start looking at these upsets as opportunities for your growth and healing, instead of ignoring them.

I've learned it often takes such emotional times to realize unhealed issues exist in the first place.

This is due to the fact that our society, for the most part, is completely out of touch with their feelings because we have not been taught how to deal with them effectively. Many of us were told not to be so sensitive or to keep our feelings to ourselves during our childhood. This resulted in us disregarding our feelings and burying them deep inside. Where do they go? Nowhere!

Feelings exist to be felt, so they can be released! Feelings are energy — and energy is meant to flow. When we don't feel our feelings, energy gets blocked within our bodies and becomes stagnant and stuck, which is dangerous to our health and possibly the safety of those around us.

Mentally, we act them out in self-destructive ways and try to escape the pain attached to those buried feelings, which often results in depression and/or addiction. Physically, the stagnant, negative energy manifests in our bodies and after lengthy amounts of time, turns into disease!

These unresolved feelings also affect others. From our loved ones, to strangers on the street, safety of others can be at risk, for when our repressed feelings finally do surface, they come out with strong force, much like a volcano which releases its pent-up energy! The results can be devastating!

So, how do we go about dealing with our buried issues? We must first acknowledge their existence, for in order to address the problem, you need to know a problem exists! Once identified, you can work through the feelings that are attached to them. I strongly believe this admission must happen in order for healing to take place, allowing the energy to be released from our consciousness! It takes courage to feel your feelings and tackle such deeply rooted issues.

When you notice yourself feeling down, and you can identify the emotion you are experiencing, I suggest voicing the feeling out loud! When you acknowledge you are feeling sad by actually stating "I am sad" for example, you will find immediately following the spoken words, the feelings begin to surface. Allow yourself time to be with those feelings and you will most likely notice, within minutes, feeling better, lighter, and back in balance. You might even experience a more positive, joyful, hopeful feeling come forward on the tail of what you have been pushing down for so long!

Another helpful tool is journaling. Journaling can help you get in touch with your feelings and gives them a voice. Simply sit down and begin writing about your feelings. You might start by writing "I am feeling sad or lonely", and then allow your hand to write whatever it wants, without judgment. I guarantee great stuff will come forward on the page!

There is something very powerful about transferring your feelings from your mind/body to the page. It helps you acknowledge and feel your feelings, which allows the energy attached to be released. I always encourage people to either tear-up and discard or burn these journal entries, symbolizing their release from your consciousness. While you do this, repeat the mantra "I release that which no longer serves me."

With this being said, what you will eventually discover is that a majority of our feelings are direct results of the negative thoughts that we used to believe were true. We now know these thoughts are not in alignment with our True selves. What we actually are doing is projecting the anger we feel towards ourselves from believing these lies, onto the outside world. Remember when this happens, self-forgiveness is needed. Fortunately, we have addressed these issues via the pages of this book, however, while you work on mastering this process, please be sure to be very gentle and compassionate with yourself.

The next time you feel your inner peace disturbed, remember that your feelings can lead to healing, the healing of the thoughts that no longer work for you and are causing you pain and suffering!

$\mathcal{A}$FFIRMATION

"I am releasing the beliefs that make me
feel anger, pain, guilt and sadness.
I am using my feelings to grow and find peace."

$\mathcal{A}$CTION STEPS

1. Practice "conscious breath work" at least once in the morning, once mid-day, and once at night. Utilize conscious breath work when you find yourself off-center.

2. Copy the suggested affirmation and post it in visible places to help you remember it throughout the day! Recite it numerous times throughout the day, and write in your journal any negative, doubtful thoughts that come up while reciting the affirmation.

3. Apply the negative core belief/thought correcting process to each, as discussed in Action step #4 in Chapter Five.

4. When you find your inner peace disturbed; feeling enraged, stressful or sad, stop and ask yourself "What belief is making me feel this way?"

5. Spend at a minimum of 10 minutes writing in your journal answering that very question for every time you experience such dis-ease.

6. Once completed, spend a few minutes acknowledging yourself for the courage to feel the feelings and then give yourself a big hug.

CHAPTER EIGHT

ARTICLE: Trusting the Process

"I am not where I want to be,
but thank GOD I am not where I used to be."

MORE THAN LIKELY, you are now realizing the things society said would bring happiness, such as a high profile career, great fortune, and material things aren't bringing you the fulfillment you expected. You have been questioning your life and are now making changes! I greatly acknowledge you for the strength and courage you are showing. Another powerful tool that will help you on this journey of removing the obstacles that get in the way of living a life of joy and fulfillment is by "accepting what is."

The process of searching for, or more accurately, discovering what you truly are here for takes time, energy and effort. Unfortunately, most human beings are lacking in the area of patience and quickly get frustrated because they aren't where they ideally think they want to be. They experience self-judgment that says they should be further along and/or feel anger and sadness because they didn't follow their heart's desire sooner. As we learned earlier, when we focus on thoughts that are self-destructive, we experience suffering. Judging what is, or isn't, is useless because it doesn't change anything, in fact, only makes things worse. The answer is to accept where you are right now and do your best to love what is. This exercise will bring us back to the present moment where peace resides, as discussed in Chapter Two.

Before we go any further, I encourage you to close your eyes and take a deep breath. Take the next 5 minutes to acknowledge yourself for the work you have done in this book to date. Repeat silently, "I acknowledge myself for the courage to walk this journey and I am proud of myself." Take time to enjoy the fruits of your labor! We simply don't acknowledge ourselves enough! How does this feel? My guess would be wonderful!

Now, let's take a moment to look back over your life. Think of a time you asked God for something and didn't get it, or didn't get it in the time frame you wanted. Then, ask yourself if you actually got what you wanted, when you wanted it, would you have been able to handle it? For most of us, the answer would be "No." We more than likely would have screwed things up because we weren't ready for it. God knows what is best for us and He/She/It will deliver it to us in perfect time, if it is for our highest good and the good of all concerned. As a wise man once stated "Thank God for unanswered prayers." God wants us to have what we desire but often times we think too small, and the greater plans involved something much bigger. So, having faith and continuing to show up for ourselves and others, is necessary!

"Accepting and loving what is" is especially important to remember while going through what I call the "in-between" periods of life. This is the uncomfortable time between making positive changes to our lives and having them actually come to fruition. We must remember that the choices we made in the past will manifest in the present and will continue to do so for a while, until our new choices take affect. If we are not thoughtful of this lag-time, we can easily get frustrated and stop our forward movement.

How you are with yourself during this inbetween period is extremely important. How are you caring for yourself when you get frustrated? How are you showing compassion for yourself when the judgments pop-up? Remember self-judgments are simply negative thoughts in disguise and you now have a process of correcting them. Practice stepping back and just observing. Remember the God of your understanding has a plan greater than yours. Learn to trust that!

One suggestion during this time is to quietly and gently repeat the following mantra when you find yourself frustrated or in self-judgment: "I have patience for the process and trust it." Another is "I am not where I want to be, but thank GOD I am not where I used to be," which gives an opportunity to acknowledge yourself for the progress you have already made while you look back to see how far you have come. Both suggestions encourage you to continue the work and motivate you to move forward.

Accepting what is allows you to accept where you are right now on your journey and practice having faith that you are exactly where you are supposed to be, which is a challenging task for many people who have not been able to trust much in their lives. I ask you to trust that through clarifying and following the desires of your heart, you will find the contentment and peace you are searching for.

I encourage you to trust the process. I ask you to trust yourself. I pray you can trust God. If you are unable to trust any of these right now, I encourage you to trust me, because I have been where you are and trusted anyway. Through trusting my process, trusting myself and most importantly, trusting GOD, not only have I survived, but now I thrive. If I can do this, anyone can! This process works!

Trust it! Trust God! Trust me!

$\mathcal{A}$FFIRMATION

*"I trust my process with ease and grace.
I am accepting and loving what is."*

$\mathcal{A}$CTION STEPS

1. Practice "conscious breath work" at least once in the morning, once mid-day, and once at night. Utilize conscious breath work when you find yourself off-center.

2. Copy the suggested affirmation and post it in visible places to help you remember it throughout the day! Recite it numerous times throughout the day and write in your journal any negative, doubtful thoughts that come up while reciting the affirmation.

3. Apply the negative core belief/thought correcting process to each, as discussed in Action step #4 in Chapter Five.

4. Before you go to bed each night, take at least 5 minutes to acknowledge yourself for the work you have done in this book to date. Silently repeat, "I acknowledge myself for the courage to walk this journey and I am proud of myself."

5. Each night before bed, create a gratitude list in your journal of at least 5 things you are thankful for. When you are appreciating what is, you cannot be focused on what isn't!

6. Whenever you find yourself in judgment or frustrated that you aren't where you want to be, repeat "I have patience for the process and trust it."

CHAPTER NINE

*A*RTICLE: Clearing Out the Clutter

"The Universe wants us to have whatever we want, but in order for that to happen, we have to make space for it by clearing out the things we don't need."

Triple A^s for the Soul

WHAT YOU HAVE BEEN DOING in this book is clearing out the emotional and mental clutter within your consciousness that gets in the way of living a life filled with joy and peace. Many people spend considerable energy on cleaning out their mental states, but don't do anything about their physical surroundings, which can have a negative effect — and vice versa.

We are now going to focus energy on your outer world, as our living and work spaces represent what is going on inside of us, and can indicate how you truly feel, or used to feel about yourself. This can clue you in on what you feel you deserve.

If you find yourself holding onto things you no longer need, that no longer serve you, or that you don't even like, you are probably operating with a belief system based on lack. Lack consciousness is based on believing that you do not deserve things, that there is not enough in the Universe for everyone, that without such "things" you are not complete or better yet, that without this "stuff" you have no worth as a human being. Allow me to set the record straight!

Clearing Out the Clutter

The Universe is abundant, it has plenty of everything for everyone; no one will go without if they take responsibility and do the work that is necessary to receive it. The Universe wants us to have whatever we want, but in order for that to happen, we have to make space for it by clearing out the things we don't need. And most importantly, we deserve all things wonderful and don't need "stuff" to make us worthy or complete — we are made Whole, Perfect, and worthy simply by being born children of God!

Hopefully, you are thinking of some area in your home that has too much clutter. Are you ready to clear it out?   Are you prepared to let go of things that no longer serve you, creating more space for other wonderful things to flow into your life? I bet you are!

The first thing to do is sit with a pen and paper and jot down the areas in your home or office that you want clutter free. These areas could be as small as a junk drawer, the space under your bed, or as big a project as your attic, garage, or basement.

Now, prioritize! Which area do you want to tackle first? Which area brings you excitement about getting done? I suggest completing this one first, for once done, you will experience the benefits of lighter living and feel energized and motivated to finish the other areas!

How do you begin this clearing process? Spend time psyching yourself up by thinking about how excited you will feel once it is completed! If it's a big task, recruit friends or family whom you enjoy being with and with whom you feel safe — you want to make this arduous task as enjoyable as possible. Get some cleaning supplies ready and create three piles: keep, donate/recycle, and trash. Then, put on your favorite music, center yourself through conscious breath work, and GO FOR IT!

Questions you might ask yourself during the de-cluttering process are: "Do I really need this? Does this bring me good feelings? Can I live without it? Have I used this in the past six months? Can someone else benefit from having it more than I?" The answers will dictate which pile the item will go on.

Clearing Out the Clutter

A word of caution; taking on such projects can be overwhelming at times. If the project is too big to finish in one sitting, set aside a few hours each week over a month's time. As you have learned earlier, having patience for the process and being gentle and compassionate with yourself while working through the necessary steps to change your life, is of the utmost important. And don't forget to BREATHE during the process!

I encourage you to tackle the cluttered areas of your life that make you feel anything less than peaceful and content. When you do, you will feel physically lighter, your work spaces will become more functional, your home environment will become more welcoming to both yourself and others, but most importantly, your outer environment will better reflect your now peaceful inner state of consciousness. As it is within, it is without!

*A*FFIRMATION

*"I release that which no longer serves me,
allowing space for wonderful things to come in."*

*A*CTION STEPS

1. Practice "conscious breath work" at least once in the morning, once mid-day, and once at night. Utilize conscious breath work when you find yourself off-center.

2. Copy the suggested affirmation and post it in visible places to help you remember it throughout the day! Recite it numerous times throughout the day and write in your journal any negative, doubtful thoughts that come up while reciting the affirmation. Apply the updating of old core beliefs process to each, as discussed in Action step #4 in Chapter Five.

3. Create a list of the areas in your outer world you want clutter free.

4. Pick one area from this list and tackle it. Once completed, acknowledge yourself for releasing that which no longer serves you and move onto the next area.

CHAPTER TEN

*A*RTICLE: Tending Your Garden

*"Some relationships are not meant to last forever;
some are here for a reason, some for a season,
and others for a lifetime!"*

Triple A^s for the Soul

GROWING UP INHERENTLY A CITY BOY in a small conservative New England town was difficult at times, but the real challenge was growing up in a dysfunctional home, a situation I am sure most of you can relate to! My parents came from challenging households and did not have a healthy concept of how siblings should relate to each other and as a result were not able to foster their children to get along. Fighting was the norm!

Through my painful and negative interpretation of the many things that happened during my childhood, I created the belief I could not trust my family. Instead of investing time and energy on them, I focused on my friendships. I chose friends who had my best interests at heart and would be there for me unconditionally. I created the belief that friendship was forever! These beliefs, which I held to be true, served me well for I have been blessed with wonderful friendships. However an event occurred years ago that challenged them!

The event involved two friends betraying me. It rocked me to my very core and left me devastated.

My world was turned upside down, as this was the one area I considered sacred and thought could be trusted without doubt. It wasn't what actually happened that was the issue, but my perception of what happened. The process that followed was extremely powerful.

This event gave me the opportunity to look at my core beliefs about friendship and re-examine my views on relationships in general. I came to realize that some relationships are not meant to last forever; some are here for a reason, some for a season, and others for a lifetime! People come into our lives at times when we need them or they need us, but doesn't mean they are going to be in them long term. Some bring forward issues we need to resolve and, if we choose, can use them as an opportunity to heal; in my case, this event allowed me to review my beliefs about relationships that no longer served me.

Even though I was thankful for my new awareness about relationships, I had to examine the integrity of these friendships. Although I realized they

didn't intentionally set out to hurt me, I asked myself if their behavior during and after the incident
was acceptable and determined it was not. I had to
let them go as friends. In my heart, I acknowledged
how much I appreciated them, how I was thankful
for the wonderful times we shared and that I would
always love them for being a big part of my life. I
then bid them peace, wished them happiness and
success, and released them!

This process, although painful, was a necessary
part of my healing journey and allowed me time to
take inventory of the relationships in my life. I not
only evaluated my friendships, but also reviewed
and discarded the irrational core belief that my
family was not trustworthy, as this was far from the
truth. I used this situation as an opportunity for my
growth and evolution and have since done my best
to use every situation I experience to go deeper into
my healing and higher into my consciousness.

I compare this experience to the process of
"tending a garden." I believe our lives are like gardens, sacred spaces that have the potential of grow-

ing beautiful things. Like a garden, we need to nurture the relationships that bring us beauty and joy, while at the same time be conscious of and perhaps release the old, unhealthy ones that are holding us back from having new experiences. We only have so much space in our gardens, so when we tend to them and clear them out, we make room for more things to grow.

During this time, I reached out to three people who were relatively new in my life that I felt strongly in my heart I could trust. I shared my sadness and hurt with them, and they loved and supported me unconditionally. When I released two people from my life, room was available for others to come in. There was space in my life for new relationships to grow. For that, I am eternally grateful.

*A*FFIRMATION

*"My life is filled with people
who nurture the Truth of who I am."*

*A*CTION STEPS

1. Practice "conscious breath work" at least once in the morning, once mid-day, and once at night. Utilize conscious breath work when you find yourself off-center.

2. Copy the suggested affirmation and place it in visible places to help you remember it throughout the day! Recite it numerous times throughout the day, and write in your journal any negative, doubtful thoughts that come up while reciting the affirmation.

3. Apply the updating of old core beliefs process to each, as discussed in Action step #4 in Chapter Five.

4. Weekly, gift yourself with a bouquet of flowers, a plant, or a visit to a botanical garden or park — something that represents the process of tending your garden.

5. Take inventory of those in your life. Create a list including all the people in your world.

6. Review your list and circle those who unconditionally love and support you on your journey. These are the people who serve as your mirror and who lovingly encourage you to take a look at yourself! These are the relationships you will want to nurture.

7. Weekly, call, write, or e-mail two people on this list and share with them how they bless your life. Express your gratitude.

8. For those not circled, begin the process of mentally releasing their influence in your life. In your heart, individually thank them for their presence in your life, bless them, and let them go.

CHAPTER ELEVEN

*A*RTICLE: Getting on Purpose

*"Happiness in life is a bi-product
of doing the things that bring you joy!"*

NOW THAT YOU ARE DILIGENTLY WORKING on removing the self-imposed obstacles; the thoughts, the relationships, and the things that do not bring you joy and have gotten in the way of fully accepting who you Truly are, it is time to "get on purpose" and begin the process of claiming and incorporating your God given talents into your life!

Remember when as children we would accidentally trip over something and out of sheer embarrassment, say to those who witnessed it, "I did that on purpose?" What did we mean when we said "on purpose?" We were saying we deliberately meant to do it! Well, everyone knows we do not intentionally trip, but we wanted people around us to think we were in control. You are now ready to apply this concept to your life!

"Getting on purpose" means living your life with intention and taking active control of it. It involves figuring out what you are here to do and then creating your own personal mission statement, which can be used as a guidepost in making future decisions!

Getting on Purpose

Webster's Dictionary defines a mission as "a sending out to perform a special duty." So, a personal mission statement defines your special duty and how you plan on achieving it. Many successful businesses have mission statements which set the bar for employee's behaviors and focus on a common goal. If it works for business, why wouldn't it work for us personally? It's time for everyone to find his or her mission and create their own mission statement! How do we begin that process?

We start by re-discovering the things we are innately good at and have passion for. Each of us is born into the world with distinct talents and unique ways of expressing them. It is our responsibility to figure out what those talents are if we truly want to be happy in life. We then can share those God given gifts with others. Notice the word "re-discovering" is used, which implies we already know what our talents are, but have seemingly, or momentarily forgotten them.

We can begin by looking at the things we loved to do, and were good at, when we were children.

What activities caused you to lose all track of time? Did you love to paint? Did you love playing with Legos? Did you love helping your mother clean the house? Did you love repairing or building things?

Take a moment now to remember those things. Allow yourself to experience the joy in this moment that thinking about those past situations brings you and write them down. It feels good, doesn't it? We knew what actions brought us joy when we were young and did them, without judgment, regardless of what anyone else said or thought. We must re-member what our inner child has always known; do what you love to do and joy will follow. Happiness in life is a bi-product of doing the things that bring you joy!

Now that you have a list of such activities, go out and DO them; buy yourself some finger-paints and paint, play with a Lego set and build, or re-organize your closets. These activities will rekindle an excite-ment within you that will help you re-discover your passions, which in return will help you define your purpose. Our passions, talents, or "gifts" were given to us "on purpose" by our Creator, so why aren't we using them to bring happiness to ourselves, and then as a result, to others?   As the late Leo Buscaglia beautifully stated, "Your talent is God's gift to you. What you do with it is your gift back to God."

Once you start remembering what brings you joy, take a shot at writing your personal mission statement. Incorporate key words that resonate with your heart, such as: love, help, heal, joy, inspire, empower. If you love to paint, try "I am here to bring beauty to other people through art." If you love to tell jokes, try "I am here to help people experience joy through laughter." Place this statement in visible places around your home and office that help you remember your purpose. Say it out loud in the morning as you brush your teeth. Use it as a guide in making decisions by asking "Is this next action in alignment with my purpose?" If the answer is yes, go for it! If not, you might want to reconsider doing it!

We learn that when we do what we truly love, others are instantly affected and we, ourselves grow!

Triple $\mathcal{A}$s for the Soul

As Julia Cameron states in her book, *The Artist's Way*, "What we really want to do is what we are really meant to do. When we do what we are meant to do, money comes to us."

Once you have an idea of your purpose, begin incorporating it into your life — either as a hobby, or better yet, as a career. If you loved playing with Legos, you might volunteer with the organization that is building your community playground, or enroll in an evening course in architecture at your local community college. Once you re-discover your passion, use your creativity to bring it to life!

Remember, you are cheating yourself, and the world, when you are not expressing your gifts! Gifts are meant to be shared and ideas are meant to be expressed!

Getting on purpose is a process of taking back control of your life! Be the person who, when asked how they accomplished something amazing says, "I did that on purpose." Not only will you have pride and fulfillment in your life, but will become an inspiration for others!

$\mathcal{A}$FFIRMATION

"I know what brings me joy,
and joyfully incorporate it into everything I do."

$\mathcal{A}$CTION STEPS

1. Practice "conscious breath work" at least once in the morning, once mid-day, and once at night. Utilize conscious breath work when you find yourself off-center.

2. Copy the suggested affirmation and post it in visible places to help you remember it throughout the day! Recite it numerous times throughout the day and write in your journal any negative, doubtful thoughts that come up while reciting the affirmation.

3. Apply the updating of old core beliefs process to each, as discussed in Action step #4 in Chapter Five.

4. Create a list of the activities that bring you joy. Incorporate them into your life NOW!

5. Create a first draft of your personal mission statement. Say it out loud every morning and let it guide your actions. Post it in visible places to help you remember it throughout the day!

6. Continually update your mission statement whenever necessary by reorganizing its order or incorporating words that more powerfully resonate with your Spirit and your intention of living your purpose.

CHAPTER TWELVE:

*A*RTICLE: Dreams DO Come True!

"If you can dream it, you can be it!"

Triple *A's* for the Soul

YOU HAVE BEEN ON QUITE A JOURNEY since beginning this book. You have faced many scary things and have completed several action steps that assisted you in removing the obstacles that got in the way of having peace in your life. Kudos to you for your courage! Make sure to acknowledge yourself for the healing that has taken place!

What's next you might be asking? DREAM!

As mentioned earlier, one of the main problems in our society is that we spend enormous time and energy focused on acquiring material things, while we neglect our personal dreams and the things that really matter in life! When we follow our dreams we find contentment, fulfillment, and joy beyond our wildest dreams. It is now time to nurture those dreams and help them come true!

What are your dreams? Often people respond with "I don't know what they are because it has been such a long time since I gave them any thought — I have forgotten them!" I am always amazed at this answer, yet I can completely relate as it was my response when asked the very same question years ago. Take note: the key to what brings you happiness in life lies in the answer! My advice is simple and clear, start remembering your dreams and then incorporate them into your life!

I encourage you to take the next few minutes to think back to a time in your childhood that was happy. Remember the excitement you felt when you were dreaming, either daydreaming by yourself, or playing with friends. Regardless of your perception of your childhood, everyone experienced moments of joy. Let me help you remember these times.

What did you want to be when you grew up? What did you want to do? Did you want to be a teacher? An artist? A dancer? Was becoming a secretary the coolest thing ever? Whatever the dream, I ask "What is holding you back from making that dream become your reality today?" At this point, we know the answer is "YOU" and your self-defeating thoughts that are not based on the Truth of who you are.

It is important to mention that some of your dreams might require things from your body that are more challenging to accomplish from when you were a child. For example, if you dreamt of becoming a ballerina, your body may no longer be able to do such an activity. Here it is valuable to revisit or update your dream to determine how you can experience the same joyful feeling and bring it forward into your life. In this scenario, it might mean creating a low-impact dance class or becoming a dance teacher!

Once you have remembered your childhood dreams, begin reclaiming them! Get reconnected to them through visualization. Picture yourself in that old, childhood dream and feel the excitement build inside as you actually experience the dream through visualizing it. Feels good, doesn't it? The very act of dreaming brings us joy — and through joyful activities we experience the happiness we are looking for. Remember, anything is possible!

With this new-found enthusiasm, create a "mind map." A mind map is a tool used to "map out" the route you will follow to have your dreams become a reality. On a clean sheet in your journal, put the date on the bottom of the page, this is where you are today. On the top, write out the destination, YOUR dream, where you want to be! Now be creative and use your imagination. Allow yourself to play and have fun! Fill in the middle area with ideas and activities that will bring you closer to living your dream and seeing it come to fruition. From this map, create a list of small action items that need to be executed to bring your dream about quicker. Do you need to take some classes? Do you need to adjust a behavior or habit? Do you need to call a friend who might be able to help you achieve your dream? Have fun with this exercise and let yourself dream — and dream BIG. Remember "If you can dream it, you can be it!" Creating this map is only the first step, however. Make sure you follow-up with action by completing the small action steps you created.

In addition, make sure to take time each day to look at your mind map and visualize and experience what the actual dream feels like. When you do this, you are activating an extremely powerful scientific phenomenon. It is proven that the mind cannot differentiate between real life experience and the ones we create in our own imagination. For example, have you ever thought of a past traumatic event in your life and immediately found yourself experiencing the same exact feelings as though it were happening all over again? The mind cannot tell the difference between which experience is "real," and as a result, it responds accordingly. If we understood the enormity of this concept, we would be more conscious of the benefits of primarily focusing on our positive past experiences.

Now, take this theory one step further by applying it to future experiences. When you focus on the dreams you want to come true, you feel positive emotion and actually experience in the present moment the dream as though it was already here, bringing you great joy and happiness. Regardless of the outcome, whether your dream comes to fruition or not, you will be happy in the present moment, and as we have learned, peace and joy resides in this moment. Furthermore, God was the one who planted our dreams within us, which means they

Dreams DO Come True!

are 100% achievable.

Make sure to enjoy the wonderful journey of having your dream come true! Don't rush it! Have patience for the process. Make sure to feed and nurture your dream like you would a pet or a plant — with love, energy, and excitement! Then sit back and joyfully watch it become reality.

Dreams DO come true and often times take work and determination on our part. Once you start this magical process of walking towards your dreams, you will realize this "work" is a true labor of love. It may also lead to other wonderful and amazing things related to or even significantly different from or better than the original dream.

So, go now and re-claim your lost dreams. Create a mind map detailing the steps you must complete. Visualize your dream, remembering the thoughts you focus on will create your life experience. Take action on those items. Help your dream become your reality. Believe it will come true. Then prepare to live a life that you have always dreamed of living. It's on its way!

*A*FFIRMATION

"Dreams DO come true."

*A*CTION STEPS

1. Practice "conscious breath work" at least once in the morning, once mid-day, and once at night. Utilize conscious breath work when you find yourself off-center.

2. Copy the suggested affirmation and post it in visible places to help you remember it throughout the day! Recite it numerous times throughout the day and write in your journal any negative, doubtful thoughts that come up while reciting the affirmation.

3. Apply the updating of old core beliefs process to each, as discussed in Action Step #4 in Chapter Five.

4. Create a mind map of your dream.

5. Create a list of small action steps that can be done to bring your dream about quicker.

6. Weekly, complete small action steps towards pursuing your dream.

7. Weekly, take at least 20 minutes to visualize your dream and experience the excitement of having it come to fruition.

8. Edit your mind map as necessary.

9. Prepare for your dream to come true.

10. Remember the thoughts you focus on create your life experience.

11. Acknowledge yourself for the work you have done throughout this book. Silently repeat, "I acknowledge myself for the courage to walk this journey and I am proud of myself."

AFTERWARD

YOU HAVE BEEN ON QUITE A JOURNEY of self-discovery throughout this book and I want to acknowledge you for your courage and determination.

Congratulations on completing this work, for as you have experienced, it is not for the weak of heart. You are now embarking on living a life without self-limitation. How exciting!

I pray this book has assisted you in remembering the Truth of who you are; a Perfect, Divine, and Whole spiritual being having a human experience. This shift in consciousness is the key to personal freedom!

Good luck as you continue on this never-ending journey called life. Enjoy the process. Thank you for allowing me to be of service to you!

Namaste!

For more information on Trent and to see how he can personally help you, visit TrentBlanchard.com.

To order copies of this book for loved ones, visit TripleAsForTheSoul.com.

Ageless Wisdom Publishing
420 North Villa Court, Suite 202
Palm Springs, CA 92262